COCOA BEACH PUBLIC LIBRARY
550 NO. BREVARD AVENUE
COCOA BEACH, FL 32931

**PROPERTY OF
BREVARD COUNTY LIBRARY SYSTEM**

COCOA PUBLIC LIBRARY
550 BRevARD AVENUE
COCOA BEACH, FL

Too Cute!
Baby Foxes

by Christina Leaf

BELLWETHER MEDIA • MINNEAPOLIS, MN

Blastoff! Beginners

Blastoff! Beginners are developed by literacy experts and educators to meet the needs of early readers. These engaging informational texts support young children as they begin reading about their world. Through simple language and high frequency words paired with crisp, colorful photos, Blastoff! Beginners launch young readers into the universe of independent reading.

Sight Words in This Book

a	from	other	too
and	have	play	with
are	in	the	
at	is	they	
each	it	this	
eat	look	to	

This edition first published in 2022 by Bellwether Media, Inc.

No part of this publication may be reproduced in whole or in part without written permission of the publisher. For information regarding permission, write to Bellwether Media, Inc., Attention: Permissions Department, 6012 Blue Circle Drive, Minnetonka, MN 55343.

Library of Congress Cataloging-in-Publication Data

Names: Leaf, Christina, author.
Title: Baby foxes / Christina Leaf.
Description: Minneapolis, MN : Bellwether Media, 2022. | Series: Too cute! | Includes bibliographical references and index. | Audience: Ages 4-7 | Audience: Grades K-1
Identifiers: LCCN 2021040719 (print) | LCCN 2021040720 (ebook) | ISBN 9781644875735 (library binding) | ISBN 9781648345845 (ebook)
Subjects: LCSH: Foxes--Infancy--Juvenile literature.
Classification: LCC QL737.C22 L434 2022 (print) | LCC QL737.C22 (ebook) | DDC 599.77513/92--dc23
LC record available at https://lccn.loc.gov/2021040719
LC ebook record available at https://lccn.loc.gov/2021040720

Text copyright © 2022 by Bellwether Media, Inc. BLASTOFF! BEGINNERS and associated logos are trademarks and/or registered trademarks of Bellwether Media, Inc.

Editor: Amy McDonald   Designer: Jeffrey Kollock

Printed in the United States of America, North Mankato, MN.

Table of Contents

A Baby Fox!	4
Out of the Den	12
All Grown Up!	20
Baby Fox Facts	22
Glossary	23
To Learn More	24
Index	24

A Baby Fox!

Look at the baby fox!
Hello, pup!

Pups are born in a **litter**. They have sisters and brothers.

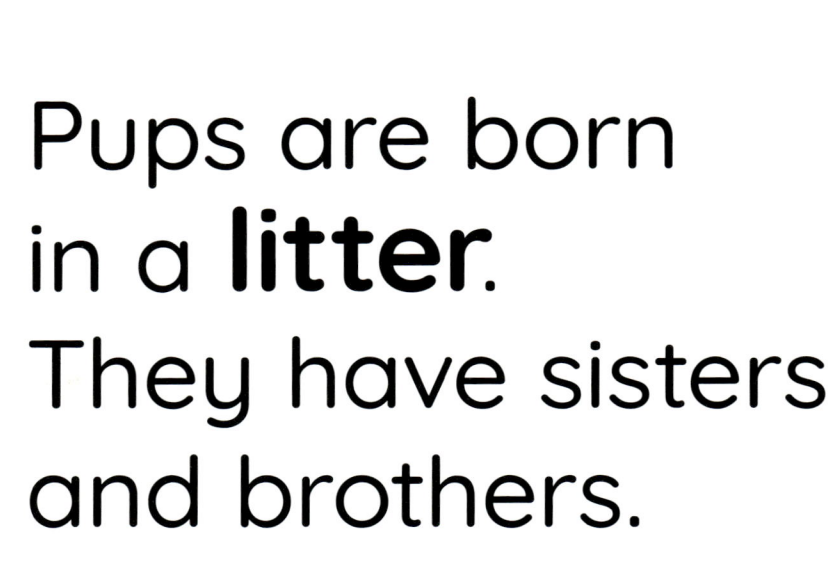

litter

Pups are born in spring. **Newborn** pups stay in the **den**.

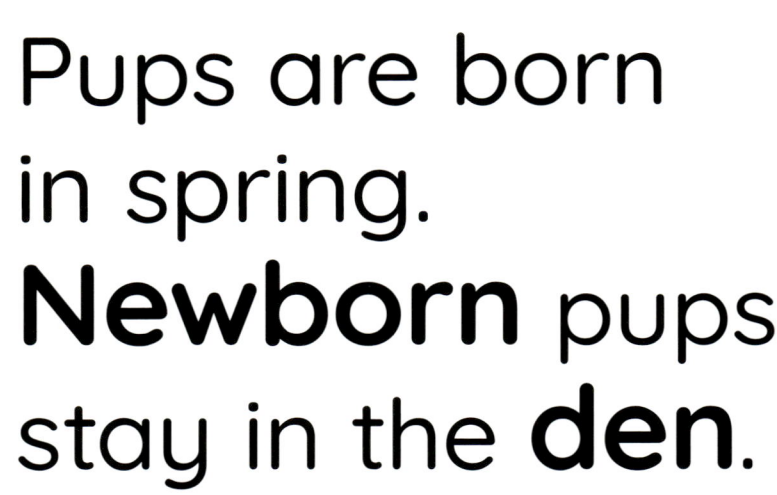

den

newborn pups

Pups drink milk from mom.
They grow quickly!

Out of the Den

Older pups leave the den. Hello, sunshine!

Pups play with each other. They **wrestle**.

wrestling

Mom and dad bring birds to eat. Pups eat bugs, too.

Pups follow mom and dad. They learn to hunt.

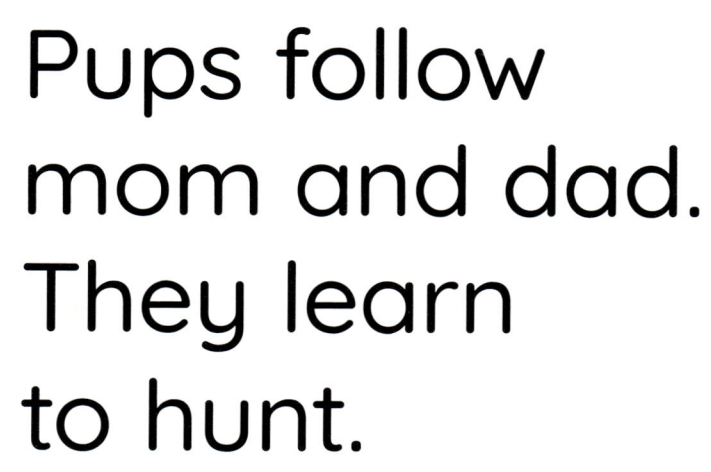

All Grown Up!

It is fall.
This pup is grown.
Bye, mom
and dad!

Baby Fox Facts

Fox Life Stages

newborn   pup   adult

A Day in the Life

drink milk   wrestle   learn to hunt

Glossary

den
a home for some animals

litter
a group of pups born at the same time

newborn
just born

wrestle
to fight by holding and pushing

To Learn More

ON THE WEB

FACTSURFER

Factsurfer.com gives you a safe, fun way to find more information.

1. Go to www.factsurfer.com.

2. Enter "baby foxes" into the search box and click 🔍.

3. Select your book cover to see a list of related content.

Index

birds, 16
born, 6, 8
brothers, 6
bugs, 16
dad, 16, 18, 20
den, 8, 12
drink, 10, 11
eat, 16
fall, 20

follow, 18
fox, 4
grow, 10, 20
hunt, 18
litter, 6, 7
milk, 10, 11
mom, 10, 16, 18, 20
newborn, 8, 9

play, 14
sisters, 6
spring, 8
wrestle, 14, 15

The images in this book are reproduced through the courtesy of: Eric Isselee, front cover, pp. 3, 4, 5, 12, 22 (newborn, adult); WildMedia, pp. 6-7; Dar1930, p. 8; Miroslav Hlavko, pp. 8-9, 23 (newborn); Jukka Jantunen, pp. 10-11; Jack Nevitt, pp. 12-13; Harry Collins Photography, pp. 14-15; Sergei Brik, pp. 16-17; Menno Schaefer, pp. 18-19, 22 (drink, wrestle), 23 (wrestle); Africa Studio, p. 20; WildlifeWorld, pp. 20-21; cynoclub, p. 22 (pup); Albert Beukhof, p. 22 (hunt); Mia Woolgar, p. 23 (den); taviphoto, p. 23 (litter).